RAKE

Matthew Caley's *Thirst* (Slow Dancer, 1999) was shortlisted for the Forward Prize for Best First Collection, and followed by *The Scene of My Former Triumph* (Wrecking Ball Press, 2005), *Apparently* (Bloodaxe Books, 2010); his 'lost second collection, *Professor Glass* (Donut Press, 2011); and his fifth collection, *Rake* (Bloodaxe Books, 2016). His work has been included in many anthologies, including Roddy Lumsden's *Identity Parade* (Bloodaxe Books, 2010), William Sieghart's *Poems of the Decade* (Forward Worldwide, 2011) and John Stammers' *Picador Book of Love Poems* (2011). He has also co-edited *Pop Fiction: The Song in Cinema* with Stephen Lannin (Intellect, 2005). He lives in London with the artist Pavla Alchin and their two daughters.

Matthew Caley

RAKE

BLOODAXE BOOKS

ISBN: 978 1 78037 281 5

First published 2016 by
Bloodaxe Books Ltd
Eastburn
South Park
Hexham
Northumberland NE46 1BS

www.bloodaxebooks.com
For further information about Bloodaxe titles
please visit our website or write to
the above address for a catalogue.

Supported using public funding by
ARTS COUNCIL
ENGLAND

Printed in Great Britain by Bell & Bain Limited, Glasgow, Scotland, on
acid-free paper sourced from mills with FSC chain of custody certification.

for Pavla –

a cellophane trumpet full
of garage forecourt flowers

i.m. Frances Caine Hobson
[1926–2012]

ACKNOWLEDGEMENTS

Acknowledgements are due to the editors and programmers of the following anthologies, periodicals, publications, websites and wavelengths where some of these poems, or versions of them, first appeared: *The Best British Poetry 2013* (Salt Publishing, 2013), *Black Light Engine Room*, www.broadcastpoetry.co.uk, *Café Review* (Portland, USA), *The Echo Room*, *Follow the Trail of Moths: The Best of Wayne Holloway-Smith's Salons* (Sidekick Press, 2013), *Haiku Quarterly*, *Modern Poetry in Translation*, *The Moth*, *Paris Lit Up* (France), *Ploughshares* (USA), *The Prague Review* (Czech Republic), Resonance 104.4fm, *Rising*, and *The Spectator*. 'Los Angeles' was commended in the Iota Poetry Competition 2009.

Nearly all the words and phrases used in 'Written Immediately on Waking' are sifted from *Les Liaisons Dangereuses* by Pierre Choderlos de Laclos.

To Mercure de France for the version from Bonnefoy. To Mr Andy Ching for wielding an erudite axe – a debt owed. To Mr Roddy Lumsden for sage whispers.

CONTENTS

Space travel's in my blood
there ain't nothing I can do about it

    THE ONLY ONES, 'Another Girl, Another Planet'

One, two and many: flesh had made him blind,
   Flesh had one purpose only in the act,
Flesh set one purpose only in the mind –
Triumph of flesh and afterwards to find
   Still those same terrors wherewith flesh was racked.

    ROBERT GRAVES, 'Ulysses'

It's beyond my control

    CHODERLOS DE LACLOS, *Les Liaisons Dangereuses*
    [Le vicomte de Valmont]

And now the dark air is like fire on my skin
And even the moonlight is blinding.
And now the dark air is like fire on my skin
And even the moonlight is blinding.

    TOWNES VAN ZANDT, 'Rake'

I was living my life like a Hollywood
But I was dying, dying on the vine

    JOHN CALE & LARRY SLOMAN, 'Dying on the Vine'

Us

Please my dearest love,
tell me of your past lovers,
you arched under them,
first one, then all together.
Hold us, think of them, and come.

The Confluence of the Elbe and the Upa

Supposedly, the
cool silver birch bole barely
two hips width shudders
like a woman on the brink
of believing in her man

They are two rivers
running into each other
clarities fusing
fast – where Coldharbour Lane runs
out into Camberwell Green

The Confluence of the Elbe
and the Upa

So, no matter that
bane flower proliferate,
cinquefoil and cress,
or silt builds scum upon scum
still they run on – sieve-panned and

as prospectors bent
to what wild seam of beryl
jasper or jade, jet-
streamed, might yet convert bedrock
into discarded jewellery –

two rivers, one back
spine-glint as a string of bulbs,
two *Pilsner Urquells*,
kinked, their quartz-strewn gravel beds
groan as the waters withdraw

14

I, fly, later slipped
the Ritzy and Railton Road
to smoke the cool lips
off Bathsheba, her moon-washed
awry realigned tank top

overlap of leaf
against leaf, veined light, networked
long-legged fly floats
arced, stilt stance on garlic bulbs
stippling estuarial banks

found a copy of
Roy Fisher's *The Dow Low Drop*
in the gutter out-
side of *Book Mongers*, leaf mulch
sailboat headed elsewhere or

The Confluence of the Elbe
and the Upa

them sank in couch grass
dew-nipped, swollen, bare-assed, blocked
tributary where
shyness meets shyness and forms
a pane of glass. Breath. Swipe. *Swipe.*

His sly cigarette.
Her furtive stretch for a book
– nipple-smudge night-smock –
Milan Kundera's *Slowness*
Modernism gone, with it

The Confluence of the Elbe
and the Upa

Skinny-dipper

Even though later
we could never get
past the slight problem of our utter lack
of rapport, we bonded then in the pitter-patter
of raindrop on lilypad, driftwood, bindweed, March violets
                    swivel-circling down the Milwaukee –

even my own idea of a river had not been wetter
than the actual suck of it as the river forgot
us, moving too fast to cling to anything, to forcefully take
the next bend, then the next beyond that, go-getter
that it was. Us, we fetched up as jet-
sam – you moss-*something*, *something*-moss, me a flung stick.

Even then I would have drunk ditch water
had it run in the rivulet
of your glistening back.

Manhole

6.00 am, Shadwell
where what the moon gifts the man-
hole is a silvered
dusting, a lid, inlaid and
anytime to be pilfered.

My Hypothetical Lovers

Have locked themselves in the bathroom
to issue only occasionally a declaration of steam,
a scroll of sinuous perfume slid out beneath the door.
They are no doubt stringing dental-floss out from the mirrored shelf
and three times around the bidet
>   *– Doto and Proto, Pherousa and Dunamene*
>   *Dexamene, Kylie and Kallianeira –*
such gurgling and slapping on the tiled floor!
This keyhole offers limited visibility. Maybe because it currently holds a key.
The hunch of a haunch, Braille. Goose pimple. Déshabillé

Alexandria will fall before they offer a share in their delightful society.
Why dally in the realm of a fool?
Two magpies land on the sweet thorn tree

outside – their laughter makes it spontaneously burst into blossom.
I know I just know they are all sharing a bath. O to be a sud on a freckled
        shoulder!

In order to hug someone properly you have to cancel yourself.

Foregone Conclusions

I *Pastime*

I had the pleasure of Jeanne Duval
somewhere between Gautier and de Banville
a few months before
she shacked up with Baudelaire.
Under the hanging tassels of her smoke-draped boudoir
off Acre Lane I lay on her, a piece of lint on a panther
and, if black can be said to shine, then her skin shone
black light, glossy, the kohl of every bone

and coiling sinew. I recall my earring caught in one of her locks,
ripping it out by the root, glimpsing its little hook.
She responded by yanking them all out – lock by lock – all fake!

yet from under them rose a massive, fabulous afro, incense-soaked as a
         thurible,
as spongiform smoke, a cloud off Bikini Atoll.
In a flash we were both exposed in negative. No one 'had' Madame Duval.

II *Little Foxes*

Long had he furtively lured
with lethal charm the little foxes back to his crash pad
off Coldharbour Lane, knowing he had not quite
eased his way past appetite
yet, or the serial use of *The Birth of Cool*
as background 'muzak', against which he stripped them bare, all squeal
         and fur-puddle
goose pimple after goose pimple
embossing sweet skin. Then came the cull

at the peak of the solo, the weld
of something wild with something wilfully withheld,
the sound of foxes – wild, urban – making out in the untamed garden

where he beheld some scared creature, yelping, making moan,
many-limbed, a snarl of assorted sexes.
Only then did he miss and moon over the little foxes.

III *My Beloved*

Madame, we will meet upon the boulevard,
alternatives being absurd,
some tree-shaded, dust-stippled kerb – in the reign of Napoleon III? –
speed-striped
horse-drawn carriages, blurred, as our backdrop. A boulevard getting laid.
The fraudulent flounce of your bustle will have me hard,
the severe cut of these breeches, starched
and staid will not impede my opprobrium. Merde!

O Eiffel, your erection casts a long shade.
Your beauty reflects in the gloss of these arcades,
the benjamin sprig at your bosom, a disrobing pomade.

You are pregnant, pregnant with the unsaid,
as I am Madame, knowing from either side of this kerb the boulevard
itself is our true beloved.

IV *Trans: anon*

O the meander-scar, continental drift
of odours
that come off her hair,
that sigh and stay, silt heavy and rare,
    hanging in mid-air

like some voluptuous air balloon – [the image predates Nadar].
I know... I have carbon-dated her nape fur,
the sibilant hem of her shift,
I have weighed each noun but look –

here he writes *O her stays, her muff*
but can only rhyme it with *if*
in her ~~dark dank sumptuous~~ rank boudoir

I have returned to, having forgotten a sock
so many epochs
after she left.

v *Foregone Conclusion*

Half-inching, then dropping down
the turquoise-pale, dolphin-studded drainpipes of the Hotel Pimodan
escaping Baudelaire's crazy demimondaine
who is pelting me with gemstones
I unaccountably land at the back of Beehive Place, Brixton, 1987,
two dealers stepping forth from their wall niche to intone:
– *how's about something beautiful to help you stay the same?* – On command
I trade a gemstone and the deal is done.

Later will find me prone
on a South London kerbstone
a lachrymose, nose-ringed fly girl battering on my breastbone
          with little fists ahead of the foregone conclusion –

my rare heart bursting like the sun,
mind half-inching up the dolphin-pale, turquoise-studded drainpipes
          of the Hotel Pimodan
tapping at the cracked window, hoping to get back in.

21

Bling

(after Baudelaire)

      My love is naked
almost, for knowing my kink
she keeps on her bling –
the piercings, tongue-studs, bangles
sounding like an *Audio-*

      slave CD through fog,
low-level tinnitus of
synths and glockenspiels
grate... I'm lasered in its loop.
It's bling as sound and lamplight,

      her cute sofa-sprawl
a laid-back 'come-on', 'fuck me
hard with your eyes' it
essays, that swart half-smile en-
larges my gorged look. Open,

      mooching languidly
she gives me the once-over
then rolls, her body
all angles, its dark delta
plays 'male' and 'female' *Velcro*

      with my gaze. Cool melts.
Those arms unkink, then legs, long
oiled and gleaming, then
that navel-pip, honey-teak
nips, blue-black Gilead grapes,

a defrocked angel.
I'm out of my tree, my chair,
detachment splintered.
Her fly boy's six-pack welded
to those lusher, lower limbs'

hard–soft construction –
Grace Jones as seen by Jean-Paul
Goude in *Photoshop*.
I turn the dimmer switch and
drain the colour from the room

leaving prinked pixels,
hard sparks to emanate from
lip, nipple, ankle,
a curveball constellation
where skin and the night are one.

Hither Green

       What led me here was
nine lines of Baudelaire in
green chalk on a door.
The hoodie fled, heels trailing
Adidas-striped after-blur

       plus, on the night bus
rail, a vibrating tine then
gold Nefertiti
brushed suede of her lower back
illumined briefly, like dusk.

Thursday and *Bladerunner* from the Rental

Thursday is salty
with firecrackers and downpour,
rain-melted neon.
With spring rolls and tiger-prawns
he flees *The Golden City*.

My Mistress Doesn't Like It When I Make Love to My Wife

So here's the angle –
sun-glaze on slant-glass roofs
such as dominate
the city in these steel-sheen
times, that well and envelop

the body. Below
elongated shadows grow
into their own re-
flections, will flood up five floors
or more. Gaston Bachelard

would stand, pause and say
'phenomenology', but
this is ghost-free build,
just the steel-slat waterfall
of escalators rising

raising human or
hologram, lifts as if an
air bubble. It's the
city as sarcophagus
of glass, cool in mirror-shades.

From up here we see
the birth of Google Earth in
a pigeon's eye
or beehives smoking off the
roofs of banks, the city a

fazed Rorschach blot on
either side of the river.
Infidelity
isn't infidelity
when it happens this high up,

        above the cloud-line
we are Gods with our own laws,
steeplejacks tip-
toe on rivet-less girders,
scudding altocumulus.

        I leave your bed, your
lain breathing body to dress,
to drain a spick glass
of *Aqua Pura*, each bub-
be as if a glass-blower

        had invested their
breath in it. The angles of
the glass give back dis-
tortions, mercury parting,
my divided attention.

The Kiss

This florist shop girl
sneaking out for a quick fag
smoke U-turning back
behind her inside the shop
to mingle with the petals.

Hat

Under this black hat
the grey paw marks of the lake
advance – soft forefoot
before hindfoot, soft hindfoot
after – look a water lynx

cleaves a clear circle
above blue serrated firs,
the clouds like coaches
stopping outside Claridges,
waves fold into each other

footmen take my hat,
epaulettes like water-reeds,
the grey paw marks move,
pine cone seen horizontal,
these watery increments

recede – hard pavements
coach wheels clack cobbles.
I have hunted lynx
amongst indexical signs,
bracken splayed and beaded but

I've not succeeded.
Neck muscles of a hunter,
slant eyes of a sphinx,
her paw marks open and close
the unvelveted waters.

This lynx guards herself
offers up prinked pawpads as
a sign in lieu of
touch, starves rib-thin and then
expects me to starve in turn.

Amongst cloakrooms where
hang ermine stoles, muffs and pelts,
the talk of Thetis
and her nymphs, new measure,
tread sure, svelte as a cat's paw,

    hat-lining velvet
hung in a London hotel,
a lake stole my mind,
her form slim as a sapling,
the sap on my hands. Bell-boy

stirs: 'Anything Sir ?...' 'My hat.'

Chamber Piece

To forswear this censer smoke in the tabernacle
for an ague in each limb,
a soft heart manacled
to the ceiling, taut knees purpled for the Lamb,
must seem as if all within her hearing
are illumined – even the sour Duchess with her muff
and chandelier-sized earrings
whose ugliness is famed as far as Düsseldorf
– illumined. His words slide inside her, as if her letter opener, the one
      with the elephant-tusk
handle, up to the hilt, the brunt
of it, electric currents
of guilt and precious pain.
If he wants her to flash her eyes whilst slyly disporting her fan
he only has to ask.

To bear the sulphurous burning of the ankles
with such casual aplomb
as if it were no obstacle
is to posit an equilibrium bordering on the numb
as if all were in the bearing –
that no matter how soiled one's shirt cuffs,
sangfroid is sown into the wearing,
for nobody can bluff the King of Bluffs
except, of course, the King of Bluffs himself. No one assesses the risk
nor accounts
for the fact that his writing has acquired a brand new slant,
which must be 'a faulty pen'
and not the narrow, freckled back of the courtesan
he has taken to using as a writing desk.

Misery Memoir

Have just finished *Les Liaisons Dangereuses* by Laclos,
the book's edge pink as litmus,
– a paper-cut!   To be run-through by a fly-leaf! –
this seep of blood, this plotting with a life
never fully known. Am laid out on this heavy-hung four-poster
with Madame de _____ and Madame de _____, mounting the very roster
of their names, their restless petticoats chime
with the riotous blossom

outside. Exhaustion is a form of exhilaration –
witness the last of any decaying nation.
His full name was Pierre Ambrose François Chodleros de Laclos,

even reading it aloud can lead us to exhaustion or a total loss
of will to ever finish a novel or anything built to last.
Excuse me while I ply my slit finger with *Elastoplast*.

Written Immediately on Waking

But first let me tell you about my gaucherie
between laurel and myrtle in the great enterprise
while tyranny is adored
and the inconsolable spouse is keeping her word
on the arm of this great spindle-shanks, surveying her injuries
imagining a pride
or at least being able to recognise
a profligate soul of the side roads –

a footman who changes into chambermaid's chic
then reads Crébillon fils' licentious novel *Le Sopha*
how perfectly suited to being a lover!

we had six hours together
folded but unsealed in a trough of sleep or panegyric
O Mademoiselle...knowledge of your weakness is my leisure.

Eridanus

      Here, the dew-pearled fern,
pier, slant shack and half-built boat
are all but tinder
for the telekinetic
arsonist – his mind elsewhere.

Her Sleepy Egypt

Where the river bed
sifts mica-chips and gravel,
dust-blue grapes ferment
upon the vine, pyramids slant
whitely, bulrushes grow out

of their own reflect-
ions, root meeting root. Meanwhile,
white, long-flanked, supple,
the High Queen mounts the divan
and settles, one bare knee raised,

kohl-eyed kiss long as
the evening, smoke-fall of her
slip, assured asp-glide.
Her mobile, set to vibrate,
starts to hum. 'Who's that?' she slurs.

'It's …'. *meep… meep…* 'Don't get
it! he rasps, taut, rebuffed, turned
off. The rival?. 'Not
now!' Ow. A great door bolts shut.
The hieroglyphics of sweat.

*

He's gone. By her wreck
of a bed, one snakeskin shoe,
Ferrero Rocher
wrapper, *Athena* poster
a smooth sunset in Cairo.

O Nefertiti
and your treacherous household.
Your eunuchs look down
as you pass. The sluice gates gush
against their ankles like milk.

A gilt-edged awning.
One clap and her maidens flee.
Sweetmeats in a cup.
If the sun is time's measure
she will surely hide from time.

I see her lower
herself gingerly onto
the spick vibrator,
the soft glove of her body
arced, her insides ribbed by sound.

Archaeology

> Duck the portal then
fuck in the sarcophagus
of expectation –
her must-breath, her dust-tipped lids.
Post-coital fug. *Big jade cat.*

Acute Hot Knee

If I behold your
rucked-up dress, revealing as
it does one acute
hot knee in all its bare-assed
actuality, nothing

is composed. My nerve
-endings blossom to a tree,
its root suffused by
a pale and horny sun, for
what divinely-revealed knee

has not sometime sparked
tercets or sestets, even,
and what sick man's mind
not fickle as an icic
-le from melt to freeze, from freeze

to…knees? More even
than the Nazarene knelt on
the watercress of
Gethsemane bewildered,
to beg, to be human, I

keep the habit of
hallucination, as the
amputee still feels
pain in their missing leg. As
white and red corpuscles cy-

cle, recycle them
-selves inside me, I try, in
vain, to out-guess, yes,
– ultimate finality! –
your divine, acute hot knee.

No

(after Corbière)

No, my sweet. Even the gaslight
knows you are sleeping fast in order to waste my night,
to hasten your exit out into clear morning
across cobbled courtyards, under the bowed awning
like fog, past Serge, our postman, who raises his cap
to you, unwittingly hailing your escape.
Back here, I try to outstare your navel,
exposed as it is by your rucked-up night-slip, utterly inimical

to a kiss. Amiss, my sweet. You are sleeping fast
in order to speed our parting, so the memory of our lust
is pushed back into the past,

a muffled cry, a mourning dove at the window ledge.
My sweet, your eyelids flicker with speeding footage –
a bleached cortège hugging the city's edge.

Buffalo Skinners

Having left M'Lady
half-naked and panting, as her husband mounted the stairs, I vaulted the
      balustrade
– preferred exit of unrepentant sinners –
dropped down to find myself in a parallel universe.

Suddenly I was a swarthy lad
exiled to New Caledonia, following the trade
of bounty hunter, each scalp a privy purse,
waist-deep in hill country, fern and furze.

*

Thus my discovery of the buffalo skinners
below a little knoll, through spruce and sumac, in a clearing,
hunkering down to scrape the skins
with their long-bladed knives – by the jangle of their spurs,
the latter betraying their position –
was relatively easy.
More difficult to furnish them with lives

or take them away. Just behind their hearing
I lay in a gulch of arch-backed ferns
each one bearing a glutinous snail with its globular horn.
They were putting bits of buffalo into a pot –
a tongue, an ear,
boiling the foulest brew. One hummed 'My Darling Clementine'. I shot
him through the left eye

the other through the oesophagus, a lasso of arterial blood veering
across the forest floor. One pine swayed, imperceptibly

*

like a woman, persistent as a melody
that lingers on the mind, a fear not allayed,
someone whose arm-span tests the width of the sun
yet is still not wide enough to steer the course

of stars. I want to fall prey to some sensational malady,
one that would prove material for several Appalachian ballads,
so sad they would fill the deepest hole within us,
each one including set-piece pines, some buffalo skinners.

Absolute Gospel

As she breathes, breathes honey into rock
or the fragrance of magnolia petals
onto a Southern wind, what gets blown back
are the husky, salient details
that make any atheist talk
as if all four gospels
were burnt onto their tongue, horde a wondrous lack
as the track ends and the train pulls

out of that slow, licentious summer,
has them instantly comprehend
why this gilt, skinny white boy stands

armed only with a tack hammer
ready to take on thousands
for a single note from Blind Mamie Forehand.

The Sleeper

Under a frothy plethora of climbing fetterbush and Virginia creeper,
the combination of three night's travel, ennui
                              and a heavy night dew
had me lain across two railway sleepers
– as once I had lain
across you – on what I trusted was a disused line,

trusted that is, erroneously. Being severed in two
only doubled my resolve to make you wholly mine.
Expect a reunion sooner rather than later.

Los Angeles

I *Modus Operandi*

> Pleasure's difficult
pain an amateur cult – so
go blame the devil
or bluff the Golden Seraph.
The fan-tailed blood-spatters on

> the pouf correspond,
roughly, with the exit wound.
The beautiful cop,
D-cup, every strand in place
moves to prove our innocence.

II *Cold Case*

> It's cool to lay here,
in my green gown, an Ice Queen
they stoop to worship.
Redheads or other highlights.
They split me like a pig's loin.

> Chrome kidney-shaped bowls.
Two pathologists argue.
A blurred rotor fan.
The rows of radial palms
outside the window. Their sway.

Low Expectation Threshold

Two buildings collapse
into flounced grey petticoats.
My earphones are in –
reformed brothers, *No Regrets*.
Padded headrest. Late-night flights.

Quaaludes

'Hey, Dude,
try these,' she whispered,
the proffered palm, the pinpoint lights, dark stars. I did.
Pines, a gravel strand. Frat boy canoodling with a co-ed.
Some cool waif approached,
said fog would afflict the Milwaukee reservoir, fed
me the falsified
warnings of high, incoming tides.
One knot of her turquoise bikini came untied.
'Au revoir, reservoir,' I feebly offered.
The first wave, a knee-high tide,

her eyes went mist, mouth seaweed.
Silt sounding, foghorns overamplified.
Everything exactly as I feared,
mud and then much more mud.
The fog level already at my head. Fog that I heard.
'Dilaudid?' she said.
'You're deluded,
it's probably *Sudafed*.
Maybe it's just the prelude.'
I kissed the mist of her head.
Fog, a corrugated shed.

A lie is the first form of need.
Eleven men in neon flak jackets veered
by a rickety pier, outmanoeuvred.
Someone said –
Quakers are odd
but often underestimated.
Fly agaric grows where a mule has peed.
I can't remember one line of Amy Lowell's 'A Blockhead'. Thank God.

There is nothing more crude
nor beautiful than a provisional study
for a Modigliani nude.

America has internalised
its own notion of jihad.
David Markson is my recommended read.
Her pubic hair was braided.
The corrugated fog was made of lead.
Wherever you go I have followed.
You, alone, have I loved.
Dark stars, lit pinpoints, swallowed,
relished then rued,
each one in the gone gut a worry bead.

Quaaludes.

Dry Land

Clearly, to be estranged from a 'bosom friend',
see their own estrangement from themselves and
                                    not be able to lend a hand
is as that man who found a mermaid inland
thrashing inside a wheatfield, parched in the mouth
                                    with beseeching hands,
rutted fields around her, mound after mound;
the ocean leagues away, status contraband,
who saw her breasts tighten at his approach, tail unwind
and thrash, the fortress of herself left to defend

which brings us to bed – the sliver of freckled back as you reach out
                                    for the lamp-stand
or a copy of _____*
so over-read its binding has come unbound

falls to the ground
in a series of serried kinks, then, brief flinch of your behind's
three swivels inside the green duvet. Lights off. Clearly, I am blind.

* possibly *Mémoire sur la captivité de Madame la duchesse de Berry*
by François-René de Chateaubriand

If for You It's Tuesday for Me It's Thursday

Coffee time-travel.
Three triple espressos fire
me two days ahead.
Tiredness is beautiful the
green world frays on its camber.

Immortality

If the blurb on the
back of Milan Kundera's
Immortality
says reading this might make you
a better lover, you might

also hazard a
lack in Nicholas Lezard
or hear yourself say
'I have just read, back to back,
Immortality, three times'

to the Creole girl
idling in the snug who yawns
licks *Rizla* papers
proclaims 'I am Miss Lemur
please don't try to impress me'

– pause – 'My favourite
flower is live forever.'
The glass collector passes
nesting glass inside glass to
scrape the ceiling. 'Time!' he says.

She: 'Profundity
is a type of ginger root
from Malabar. I
named my child Profundity,
it might be yours.' Pause. More pause.

Infinite hindsight
means that to forgive is to
forget so after
three centuries her features
begin to blur. I forget.

Crowd-babble and froth
muffle the jukebox so words
get erased – only
bass lines hurt your shoe soles in
the bling of ice and optics.

'Profundity and
me?' I say. 'No way'. 'Time!' says
the barmaid, curtly.
We file out into drizzled
spring, smelted tarmac, taxis.

Miss Lemur says 'Bye!'
the royal road behind her.
Seersucker   draft-lines
ripple past iron railings
a scarf of slaloming smoke

Immortality
left on a bar-room table
one *Rizla* marking the page.

Gursky

      The kerbstones by the
neon-lit laundrette smell of
Daz, *Omo* or *Dreft*.
You light a roll-up; above
DLR trains float through glass.

The Funicular

I am the man who
rides the funicular up
and down, livery
grey-green, and rising above
the urinals, the arbor-

etums, the cloud-line,
down and up, feeling like a
Venn Diagram or
one out of sorts with the Law
of Torts, above bread smells from

the boulangerie,
the neon-green signs of the
pharmacists, I see
further than anyone, far
into their pupils and out

the backs of their heads.
Wednesdays list up and down,
then Thursdays the same.
I have not been in love with
a ticket collector since

funiculars were
all fully automated.
Repetition is
action, repetition breeds
willpower and willpower

breeds the rare – *voilà!*
as here, these pigeons, this air
made for each other
me and this funicular
in its green-grey livery.

AM's I am grey,
liverish, usually
a filter coffee,
some Pléiade edition
then to the funicular

to take the angled
air, upward or down, down there
to keep my place in
the text with a vexed stare – yawn –
with De Beauvoir or Sartre.

'To read is to be
laughed at by the dead,' they said
once, riding the fun
-icular from leaf-vein to
stone step to fine-veined leaf and

'To erase, to be
denatured,' that's the thud of
this funicular.
'To read is to revise, to
betray your own insides, to

people your own sol-
itude' – my funicular
sidling into the
future. I go down, then rise
through grey-green skies, pigeons,

and know that to read
is to be lead into an
orchard by André
Gide and be buggered by three
florid Dukes. Yes I know this,

I am the man that
rides the skyline of Paris
in the green funicular.

The Boulevardiers

Here they come, the boulevardiers, down the avenues
past the piles of horseshit, upturned tables, blistered plane trees,
each with their turtle on its sky-blue leash, each bearing in their lapel
a curt sprig of mistletoe or myrtle
from the Bois de Boulogne, they pass in twos and threes yet will not yield
the highway. They intend
to forestall the growth
of a great city, as likely, alas, as stopping every blossom bud from putting
        forth

or torchlight deflecting off a riot-shield.
One bows to a Duchess and his head falls off. Yet still they pass, in threes
        and twos
each single-shot lapel bearing its spray of forget-me-nots or flax,

with their fertile talk and their calf-cut trews trailing the lay-bys,
their turtles fanning out on sky-blue leashes, in turtle slo-mo, so I still have
        their backs
retreating down these avenues.

The Giantess

(after Baudelaire)

Back then when Madame Nature, driven to horny excess
was shelling out feral kids by the dozen
I'd like to have been shacked up with a young giantess,
a tame cat beneath the largesse of 'my Queen'.
To watch her body and mind become full-grown
through playing hide and seek or – *warmer, warmer* –
to read the sheen in her icy chrome-brown
eye as a sexy, wavering flame.

To explore her form at leisure as she starts to doze
off, abseil up or down one stupendous knee,
try an inner thigh, then, as oppressive September ramps up the degrees

lie upon her bosom, feel as infinitesimal
as a greenfly landing upon a cathedral
below which whole cities sleep in a quite lull.

Ice

Vodka and ice *sans*
ice. The tepid choose morals
or sit under trees.
Nine glockenspiel icicles.
We kiss in the Ice Motel.

Walnuts

    Then the heatwave flinched
and trees arched upward as if
replenished when your
brown eyes tried   so haltingly
to withhold a   withhold a

        tear and their surface
-s pearled darkly for about
one microsecond,
then dried. You told me about
your grandfather, walnut groves,

        graves. My duty to
cave in to need, cave into
beauty at any
opportunity, but you,
you flirted with the waiter

        and the five tines of
your fork lit up the rood. Then
the tear retreated
– your half wipe could not have been
lighter – but inside you were

        irrigated as
after a long drought by a
dew so wet it would straighten
out the wrinkles on a wal-
nut to a tabletop. I

would have you in a
white vest, ravish you on that
table covered in
walnuts. Excuse me. I would
be dishonest with you but

for this shimmering
night and all propriety
outlawed. There, that's said.

Cloud Catcher

Your eyes weighted me
chrome-brown, one slightly awry,
   [– *they said none of them could see* –]
as the kite string weights a kite.
As a cloud in a rear-view
mirror I am seldom caught.

Your mind vetted me
earring of chalcedony
   [– *they said none of them could see* –]
somewhat time-worn shirt
As a cloud in a rear-view
mirror I am seldom caught.

Your look baited me,
Venice-print dress all at sea
   [– *they said none of them could see* –]
and me seeking port,
As a cloud in a rear-view
mirror I am seldom caught.

Your eyes netted me,
chrome-brown, one slightly awry
   [– *they said none of them could see* –]
all that could be sought.
As a cloud in a rear-view
mirror I am seldom caught.

Plane Tree Outside the Ritzy

my shoulder was born
as your flaking bole was born
to prop the other
up; crowds leave a cinema
become lights in your branches

it's as if you have
sucked up all their films like sap
documentaries
of veined leaf-light, vein-streaked bark
seething through your filaments

all those back-stabbings
punch-ups   *perruques*   prosthetics
slow-motion flying
each popcorn piece enlarged
to a *Sensurround* Big Bang

as they leave blinking
at the great, dropped screen of night
all its long-shot extras
unnoticed – that's you and me –
the plush threshing at your height

they stare at mobiles
they text into nothingness
outstare their trainers
do not clock our mutual
lean   propping each other up

they climb Brixton Hill
their heads dizzy with trailers
the cinema shuts
we become our own cold lights
we wrap the night around us

       I smoke your rolled leaves
lint   aphids   in a street-swirl
cradle a manhole
where side by side Coldharbour
Lane lies down with Railton Road

       our orbiting thoughts
so interplanetary
everywhere, there
a wheeze   somewhere poor Guy Fawkes
goes out in a spurt of sparks

       bone of my shoulder
streaked bark of your stolid bole
fusing   and lights in your branches

Laundrettes at Night

...still the whole city
often I long to break in
coin-up all machines
to shudder ...watch pantaloons
slop and cartwheel endlessly

notes for **The Plateaux**

I

     On an isthmus un-
able to lift itself out
of the zinc-grey surf,
unmotivated nomads
wait on continental drift,

II

I have seen horses sing off-key,
              green leaf within green leaf
     a perfect symmetry, but met no one coming my way
          carrying a copy of Louis Zukofsky's '*A*';
not by the Recreation Centre, *Bon Marché*
     or the lights hung in the tree outside the Ritzy
has anyone come my way
     carrying a copy of Louis Zukofsky's '*A*';
I have seen what the endoscope can see,
     the sweet blue sea,
          steel instruments on a tray
but rarely, if ever, has anyone come my way
     carrying a copy of Louis Zukofsky's '*A*';
          I have heard goats cough at the blue sky, a wan sun,
workers ostracise workers from the party,
     but never, coming my way, anyone resembling anyone
          carrying a copy of Louis Zukofsky's '*A*'.

III

Along the line of a zinc-grey, low-lit corridor
one is drawn to the glow-
ing square replete with backlit attendant, where
you will discover the lost property room of the crumbling opera
house, stuffed as it is with so many unclaimed boas,
binoculars and *pince-nez*, a
realm of brass rails and feathers.
Once there, ask in demotic French for Monsieur Drellard's curio-
umbrella, sign for it and go.
This you may know as
the plateaux.

Equanimity

Of this buckskin stallion
tethered to a silver birch
whose nostrils flare and arch,
first breath a plume, then a tower, then a frisky dragon,
who tugs his halter for sheer ebullience,
kicks the mute snow piles so they smoke and steam,
who ruts and strains – not much more can be said
except to tether you to this bed

with knotted kerchiefs trussed from each iron
bedpost and apply the birch – one tender touch –
equidistant as we are from the nearest whiskey den due west of here and
        the nearest whiskey den

due east, to thrash out the last strains of occasional brilliance.
As for that Spanish galleon
its prow is shedding gold on your dilapidated porch.

Arboretum

I *Bay Laurel*

Post-carnival, who could imagine this bay laurel
not being sunk in a water butt,
but clung to a limestone precipice, rugged of root,
nuzzled by air scented with Florence fennel
all around it, air that will soon release to us, serial gust after serial gust
as if on schedule, in vials
or capsules,
the indisputable pheromones of lust

and, occasionally, love? No one. No, my one quarrel
is not with this bay laurel, nor your bravura
strip in the gatecrashed honeymoon suite, mesh knee-stockings off, green
        afro off, long thin back unsleeving from its sheath

shoulders, stars, feint welt of bra-wire
then below, but with that callow bell-boy kneeling at the keyhole
may he suffocate upon his long-held breath.

II *Fruit Tree*

And so it was, darling, in withering rain, somewhere down by Millbrook
        Road, Brixton
that a rain-bent plum tree dumped
a half-ripe plum
on my head, inducing brief pain
but no revelation, unless you count my affected vision;
plum trees by a lake
where a white schooner creased the surface
tension, a tension that failed to break

the resulting wistful streak
worthy of Nick Drake
when I supped each night at Loughborough Junction, in the nearly burnt-
    out *Green Man*

with 'Mary Jane' and 'The River Man'
careering back each time, in withering rain, to Millbrook Road – *no mill,*
        no brook, no road – a small, soft contusion
growing under my hair. Apply other analogies if you think I've skimped.

III *Willow*

If you ever felt the fallout from an arc of welding-sparks
or bent at a burst of fireworks
then you might be able to muster a touch more empathy
as to what it must be like
to lie in its filtery lee
by the boating lake of this shabby municipal park
doing nothing, almost blissfully. But I know you haven't and therefore
        won't and lack
the gift of telepathic sympathy. You disappoint me.

They have bent towards water through history,
                    since the days of the ark,
their shady influence spreading, their leaves typically
sad but soothing sparks. This one bends to a dank culvert
                    and a concrete bulwark.

A flask of filter coffee, *The Collected Works*
of Percy Bysshe Shelley, who knew this one as a sapling, knew me.
You might even see the mistletoe at its height, if your lenses were in and
                    it wasn't so dark.

68

IV *Orchard*

Darling, take a bite out of this perfect, freckled apple
and if these words
don't turn it into an orchard
nothing will,
believe me. A fly-pecked, electric-fenced, dappled
orchard at that, where a foam-flecked horse has its reins caught up in the
        blossom, braying hard
and tossing its wild-eyed head
– the apple tree as tourniquet – tamping down the topsoil

at each twist, turn or pull. Intervene. Your words might then hold sway
with me, as leaf-shade
holds sway with an aphid

so either the poor horse strangles on its tree
or gains its liberty with a sudden windfall
if blossom can be seen to fall at night. Darling, take a bite.

V **Palm**

Like him, boredom is viral; as rain
on the sills, on the cars,
which still fan
out underneath its garrulous ribbons, the fine, feeble bars
of it drilled with no little intent. Under his cornsilk hatband, the Great
        European,
in obligatory cane chair
fares better than the other scurrying citizens –
his espresso, if seen from the palm, a tadpole seeding the ovum of the
        table, for

though boredom is inverse stage fright,
waiting in its own wings, self-prompted and second-guessed,
boredom is also vivid – a rondeau

of nothingness writ;
into which steps the rain-soaked, flagrant waitress,
adjusting her bright green bandau by the Gare du Nord.

The Young Hegelians

Supposedly the
River Neva disperses
the waters of Lake
Ladoga into the Gulf
of Finland, through the Baltic

sea, and might be the
site for a purge of leaders,
looters in foodhalls,
an awning frozen to a
portcullis of icicles.

We sat, shiver-still
discussing dialectic
like any group of
Prussian intellectuals,
Hegel, *A Hegel Reader*.

We were either side
of that chill sea, gin soda
grey interference
yet your eyes – black flaw in green,
green flaw in black – made me thaw.

Wind that could rend a
windsock made your own voice seem
as if coming through
a vocoder, though you stood
next to me, trying to sell

some bootleg CDs
to no one, *echt*-Phil Oakey
gone solo produced
by Giorgio Moroder
your eyes like sloes against snow.

We knew history
has no coda but sings in
our ears on shuffle,
incessantly on shuffle
like wind through a cracked windbell,

knew the stilled Neva
would disperse Ladoga's drift
into the Gulf of
Mexico, turn fumarole
make green vegetation steam.

*

Later, warmed by the
radio in your Skoda
you would show me the
petrified shopping malls and,
beautiful on the open

road, police-horse drop-
pings frozen into snowballs.

The Salamander

(after Yves Bonnefoy)

Any salamander, come upon, goes motionless
then plays dead. That's how a stone nurses its first thought,
that it might grow into consciousness,
a seer of flame, a start.
This salamander's half way up
the fridge, amongst the magnets, basking in the heat
from the window opposite. Its contact lens lime green with a black stripe,
unseeing, though I see a little pulse beat-

ing at the side of its head. You are pure fridge door – my riddle, my
        puzzle, my mate –
how I love you for compressing so much into silence,
solar power turned inward, reduced to its very essence.

How I love you for taking all the stars of the universe
as your body cells, love you who patiently wait upon the prize,
your breath held in, your toes in the dirt.

Afterglow

(after the Czech of Ferda Mravenec)

Asleep they seem so innocent, these concubines,
arms around each other, kohl-
etched care-lines
all smoothed out, recent flexible sins annulled.
I lie a little to one side, the forgotten man,
left hand issuing smoke, smoke that stays and curdles
                              between stained ceiling and stained ceiling fan
while the grate's embers exhale, imagining them way back, as children
shrieking at ocean spray, the wetted hem of the tideline

rinsing everything. No one else would admire them
so in slumber
or calculate the rate

at which their eyelids vibrate
at dawn's first guilty blush. No one. No one else would hum
them this lullaby under the freshening thunder.

Alacrity

    Flee the bordello
naked down the fire escape
light through a lime tree
dissolving time into wisps –
zinc greys, mostly, and yellows.

The Hammock

What wind so blew that
a hammock netted a man?'

ANON

Two silver birches
bear the burden, which after
all is only some
diamond shapes of air defined
by diamond-shaped hemp or twine

a man might fall through
somewhat strained, to the hard ground,
the upended sky,
the garden more of a slum,
fallen plums, rhubarb ditches,

guy-ropes, trashed hutches,
to swing between states – high, low –
as if borne by the mind, fill-

ing a space he has
left behind, bearing no weight,
parched ground, hard-cut slants of light.